THE NEED TO KNOW LIBRARY™

EVERYTHING YOU NEED TO KNOW ABOUT
DIGITAL PRIVACY

COLIN WILKINSON

Rosen
YA™

New York

Published in 2018 by The Rosen Publishing Group, Inc.
29 East 21st Street, New York, NY 10010

First Edition

Library of Congress Cataloging-in-Publication Data

Names: Wilkinson, Colin, 1977– author.
Title: Everything you need to know about digital privacy / Colin Wilkinson.
Description: New York : Rosen Publishing, 2018. | Series: The need to know library | Audience: Grades 7–12. | Includes bibliographical references and index.
Identifiers: LCCN 2017002119| ISBN 9781508174004 (library-bound) | ISBN 9781508173984 (pbk.) | ISBN 9781508173991 (6-pack)
Subjects: LCSH: Internet and teenagers—Juvenile literature. | Privacy, Right of—Juvenile literature. | Computer security—Juvenile literature. | Internet—Moral and ethical aspects—Juvenile literature.
Classification: LCC HQ799.2.I5 W55 2018 | DDC 004.67/80835—dc23
LC record available at https://lccn.loc.gov/2017002119

Manufactured in China

CONTENTS

INTRODUCTION

After hearing of a new movie becoming available on the streaming service Netflix, a friend of yours decides to sign up so you both can watch it. To create an account, he needs to use an accessible email address that can respond to any activation notices. The friend needs to enter a password to access the service. Finally, your friend provides information for a parent's credit card, including the billing address. Once the friend finishes creating the account, he can also spend some time selecting preferences and adding movies to the list to watch later.

In the span of ten minutes, Netflix has been provided with a large amount of personal information. The company now has payment info, including credit card, name, and address, on file to bill the subscription. It also stores an email address and a password. That's not all, however. Netflix also knows what types of content your friend prefers to watch, when he watches, what devices are used to watch, and where he is watching from. All of this information is stored and analyzed to provide Netflix subscribers quick access to the movies and shows they're most likely to watch.

Your friend provided this information willingly, and Netflix is a trustworthy service, but what if this were a less reputable website? How would your friend's actions and willingness to register for an account differ? Is there a privacy policy, and did your friend read it? There is no

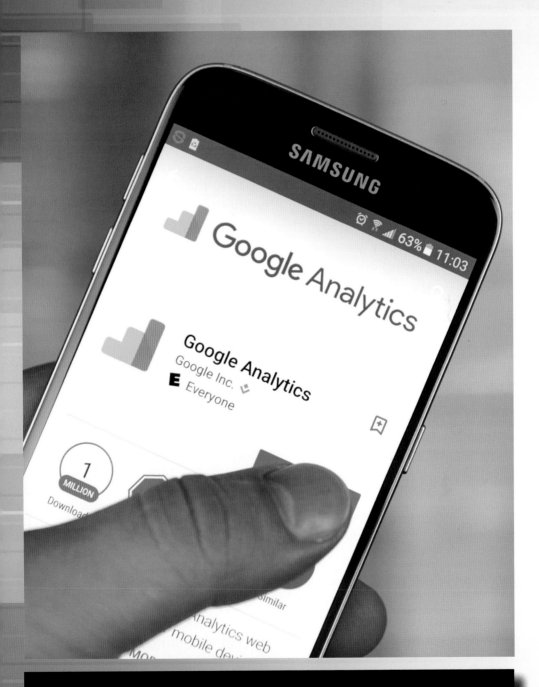

Data tracking apps like Google Analytics gather and evaluate insights on how people interact with websites, apps, and even the world around them.

way to know for certain if Netflix, or any other site, stores the provided information securely. It's possible that a site might gather and sell usage information, which other agencies can use to market their services. Consider that most interactions made online employ similar tracking techniques, often without the user realizing it. Apps and websites that may not accept billing information can still gain access to personally identifiable information. They might use your tracked data to make educated guesses as to how and when you will use their service and what ads it should show when you do.

Every year, our consumption of online media takes new shapes, and this consumption is increasingly interactive. What one might assume is a passive, one-sided experience has fostered a big industry of data tracking and analysis. Whether it's navigating a website, messaging a friend over a social network, using an app on your phone, or making a purchase, someone out there is interested in what you are doing. While much of this data is stored and used anonymously, and with good intent, there are those who would use it nefariously to steal information about credit cards, online accounts, or even identities.

As fast as the technology we rely on to make our lives more mobile and convenient advances, so too do the tools for using it safely and privately. The dangers that exist are why it is important to explore what it means to take part in today's digital world, know how data is recorded, and proactively work to keep it safe. There should be a plan for when these safety checks fail and how to recover from digital privacy intrusion.

CHAPTER ONE

LIVING ONLINE

Today's internet has come a long way from its humble beginnings in the early to mid-1980s. Although the groundwork for the internet can be traced back to efforts as early as the 1960s, home access wasn't available until much later: it wasn't until the mid-1990s that dial-up access became commonplace across America. In fact, the number of Americans subscribing to an online service provider more than doubled from 1994 to 1995. In just a few short years after that, more than half the country was accessing the internet regularly.

At the same time, online shopping was beginning to emerge. As early as 1994, the internet provided users the ability to make purchases without having to leave the house or pick up the phone.

Many online activities had their start way back then, if not before: chat rooms and forums, news and gossip sites, online games, and eventually social sharing services quickly became popular with the online community. Seemingly overnight, the world became connected and was sharing information at a level never seen before.

Today, the internet reaches beyond computers to mobile and wearable devices, appliances, and cars. A connection no longer requires a phone line, and many urban areas provide free Wi-Fi. Cell towers create a web across the landscape to maintain a continuous connection. There are structures in place to keep these tools safe, including privacy measures users can control, and they evolve just as quickly as technology does.

A DAY IN THE LIFE

Defining and enforcing what privacy means today includes considering how we're accessing the internet, whether that's from a computer or smartphone or television, what we're choosing to do online, and what agreements we make with the businesses with which we interact. In an average day, one might check the weather online to decide what to wear, listen to some streamed music while on the bus, and send a text message to a friend or parent to plan an after-school activity. While in school, one might look up a reference from a computer in the school's library, and later, one might end the day watching a streaming service, playing an online game with friends, or chatting on a favorite social network— all without considering just how much information is shared to make those connections rewarding.

As more of our lives are being spent online, we create more opportunities to be exposed to cyberbullying, cyberstalking, identity theft, and similar malicious attacks. Younger generations spend more time socializ-

BY THE NUMBERS

Internet usage has grown at an increasing pace since access became available in the 1990s. It is estimated that less than 1 percent of the world's population had access to the internet in 1995, whereas today that number has grown to 40 percent. Within that span, it took ten years to reach one billion internet users in 2005. In 2010, the second billionth user was reached in half that time. It took even less time to reach three billion users in 2014. Though the rate at which new users are gaining access to the internet is slowing, we're well on our way to four billion.

These are some of the early personal computers. As they became more accessible and commonplace, so, too, did the desire to connect them to the online world.

(continued on the next page)

> *(continued from the previous page)*
>
> In the United States, an estimated 88.5 percent of the population had access to the internet at home in 2016. This access has been aided by the penetration and popularity of smartphones and similar connected devices and the on-the-go convenience they provide. In 2015, 7 percent of smartphone owners used their phone as the exclusive means for accessing the internet. That number continued to rise to an estimated 11.7 percent in 2016 and is projected to rise to 15 percent by 2020.

ing online than adults, a trend that is likely to continue. Maintaining a healthy approach to living online requires attentiveness on the part of the individual. While laws do exist to protect users, they can be challenging to police.

CATCHING UP WITH PRIVACY ONLINE

Existing laws were poorly equipped to handle the online revolution. Privacy concerns began to arise long before regulations could catch up. But in time, the US government was able to respond to the various threats that came from online predators.

ADJUSTING TO THE WEB

The Privacy Act of 1974 was enacted decades before internet usage became common. Later accompanied by the Electronic Communications Privacy Act of 1986, these guidelines for how personal information can

Congress is one branch of government tasked with modernizing the many regulations concerning privacy so that they conform with the reality of how people use technology.

be collected and used were grossly outdated by the 1990s. In essence, these laws define and place limits on surveillance by federal agencies of the US government. Though they do cover electronic communications, including some financial transactions, they were not written with online interactions in mind. In fact, it wasn't until 2005 that the Electronic Communications Privacy Act of 1986 was extended to include email messages in transit. Since the responsibility for policing these activities was largely absent, such supervision often fell to advocacy groups.

At the same time, home connections to the internet were becoming vehicles that facilitated the rise of identity theft, thanks to storing and transferring information on computers. These thieves no longer had to dumpster dive to obtain personal information. Online media and interaction was a new playing field, with no best practices and little education for users on how to participate safely. Users did not always know what to expect or how to identify an ill-meaning website or email. Even creating an online account and password was new for most users, who had no understanding of password strength.

As the internet and its usage evolved, so did the tactics used by those looking to compromise the privacy

EDWARD SNOWDEN

In June 2013, Edward Snowden released thousands of classified documents from the National Security Agency (NSA). The files, gathered while he was working there as a contractor, revealed surveillance operations being run by the government against the American people. The surveillance efforts, ruled unconstitutional later that year, were shown to be administered with willing assistance from telecommunications companies and other governments.

The data being recorded included email and text message content, cell phone location data, and contact lists. The documents also revealed that the government was able to access data directly from large service providers, including Yahoo! and Google, and view personal user account information.

These leaks turned the attention of not only Americans but the whole world toward digital privacy and security concerns. Snowden's efforts exposed major security holes throughout some of the largest internet and communications companies, as well as in federal government agencies. The NSA, thought to be on the cutting edge of cybersecurity, had nearly two million classified documents stolen without realizing it. In the years that followed, Americans have been less trusting of online shopping and banking and have demanded more transparency from websites on their privacy practices. This increased awareness of online privacy risks has prompted major online businesses to regularly release transparency reports detailing these types of information and legal requests made by various agencies around the world.

After leaking national security secrets to the press, Edward Snowden has been in hiding in Russia and has only appeared to discuss his actions over video.

of its users. In the mid- to late 1990s, spyware became prevalent. Early on, spyware was used to better strategize marketing efforts by collecting usage information. Its purpose was turned to stealing information from users and recording their activities with greater depth. Spyware and similar harmful software quickly became more aggressive, transforming into tools for identity and digital finance theft. This created a new demand for antivirus programs to protect against these threats. The need for antivirus software continued to grow, and it is now included on most devices in some form or another.

IDENTITY PROTECTION

In 1998, Congress adopted the Identity Theft and Assumption Deterrence Act. The act allowed federal law enforcement agencies to investigate suspected identity theft and fraud, and it paved the way for more policies revolving around online content and information. Previously, only financial institutions could be considered victims of identity theft. This law expanded the definition to allow individuals to be considered victims as well.

The same year, the Children's Online Privacy Protection Act of 1998, more commonly known as COPPA, was enacted to regulate the collection of user data from minors under age thirteen. The law has evolved over the years and has become the driving factor behind websites and apps requiring children to obtain parental consent before creating an account. The law also

User tracking and data gathering can be thrown off when there are multiple users for one device, especially if they are different ages.

formalized the ability for approved organizations to self-regulate within their industry. These so-called safe harbors include online privacy and advertising groups as well as the Entertainment Software Rating Board, the group that determines video game content ratings.

In addition to federal legislation, a number of states have further refined what privacy in this day and age means and where its limitations lie. In many cases, the state laws act as an extension to the groundwork laid at the federal level. They can provide additional focus and can sometimes react to the rapid changes in modern technologies more directly to remain current.

CHAPTER TWO

YOUR DATA, YOUR PEACE OF MIND

In between classes, you pull out your mobile phone and check in on your favorite social network. Scrolling through your feed, you see a post from a friend that reads, "Can't wait until lunch!" Feeling a bit hungry, you tap to show you like the post and continue scrolling until you see another friend has posted a screenshot from a video game you have been playing. Tapping to enlarge the image, you realize your friend is farther along than you, so you add the comment "Hey, no spoilers. ;)" before tossing the phone in your bag and heading off to class.

These types of interactions are pretty common and may seem trivial. The fact is, you have just shared information that online networks and advertising services would find helpful. You've also shared some personal information that could be used against you.

DATA WORTH SHARING

In the example above, the interactions that stand out the most—that is, the data that you choose to share and make public—can lead to active data collection.

A history of content shared over social channels can go into predictions and assumptions about what someone likes to engage with and share.

In this case, your shared actions include liking that your friend is hungry and your worry over your other friend advancing too far ahead in a video game. Anyone viewing your social page listing your recent actions can clearly see both of these items. It is also easy to share more sensitive data, such as a time and location for meeting with a friend or your phone number so your friend can get in touch. Although the intended audience may be your friend, others might be able to view your message if you have selected the public sharing setting. This data can also be stored permanently as part of a digital footprint and would then be available to the app for future reference.

YOUR DIGITAL FOOTPRINT

Each time you go online, you leave a trail that is similar to real-life footprints. Each website visit, link click, account log-in, and access of streaming media can be recorded as part of your digital footprint. Everything you put on the internet and everything you request from it goes into your digital footprint. Each part of this trail can be made public and shared and can become available to be searched. Once a digital footprint is made, it may become a permanent testament to how you have behaved online, what you have reacted to, and how you responded.

Be aware that businesses may view social profiles and other aspects of someone's digital footprint before choosing to hire the person. Similarly, college admissions often review the online activities of student applicants. Even going to see a doctor can contribute to a digital footprint. There is now a legal requirement for medical records—which contain many facets of confidential and private information for basically anyone who has been to a doctor—to be stored digitally. These changes require similar, or even more advanced, changes in how we protect and ensure protection for this data. There has already been at least one major public exposure of personal medical records discovered, and it is likely not to be the last.

Changes to a part of a digital footprint may not completely cover up any previous content. So when sharing

Digital medical records are easier to look up than a paper filing system like this one. There are many other pros and cons to storing data in each way.

(continued on the next page)

(continued from the previous page)

or accessing different websites, it's safest to act like there's someone looking over your shoulder. Maybe it's a parent or your best friend. Would you want to share your activity with them? Would you be embarrassed, or would they be offended if they found out what you are writing? When taking actions online, always consider your digital footprint.

There are also some hidden aspects of what happens when accessing a website. To start, the site records the access date, the length of access, and possibly the user's location. It's possible that the app records what items the user scrolled past in the feed, perhaps as an indicator of content that did not interest the user. This data gathering is completed with users' best interests in mind and usually with users' expressed consent when they agree to an app or website's privacy policy.

Behind the scenes, more data is moving between the device and the app's servers. The app shares some form of account information to prove who the user is. And the data is flowing through the internet, routed through a web of servers across the country to reach its final destination. In order to reach the internet, a user's phone initially broadcasts the data to a cell phone tower or wireless internet network. Even the act of accessing the app to begin with might require some form of password to unlock the phone. Each of these steps offers a level of security that is essential to maintaining privacy online.

OUT OF SIGHT, OUT OF MIND

Personal information and activity is at risk not only while in transit. All of this information needs to be stored in order to be analyzed or referenced at a later time. This might be on the app's servers or perhaps on storage provided by another service used by the app. Some information might be stored locally within the app, right on the phone. In reality, it is probably a mix, with some data being stored locally while the bulk of it is stored across various servers.

Different data will be recorded to different locations, depending on who is requesting the information. Ideally, any log-in and account info would only be stored by the app and its servers, and hopefully in a format that ensures it is encoded so that it is not directly readable. Other information, however, might be stored to servers maintained by an ad delivery service. Some information will be retrieved and stored by external analytics providers. It's likely this data would be stored in more than one location, making it faster to retrieve when needed and to protect against crashing systems. These actions are never announced to the user.

WHAT'S THE RISK?

All information gathered from your online activities can be used in a variety of ways. An acceptable use for gathering data from a social media user might include

Modern phones allow users to engage in social activities, gaming, research, and more from nearly any location at any time.

choosing to show more posts from the friends with whom you interact, while hiding activity from others. Perhaps the app includes advertisements for games similar to the one you commented on. Or maybe the app would make recommendations for a good place to eat nearby. These are all helpful and acceptable features that make apps and websites so popular. In effect, we trade some privacy for this convenience.

Some of this information might be shared persistently with other apps or sites. While still acceptable usage, this does increase risk and can feel intrusive. For instance, a video game site might suggest tips and tricks for the game you originally commented on—in an unrelated app. Even more likely, the private interactions made on the social app might become public when shared by a friend or when the app updates its functionality. Although you didn't share anything negative, perhaps the circumstances of timing—you shared it in between classes, for instance—is something that can get you in trouble. A more blatantly unacceptable usage might be to sell your personally identifying information to a third party for the purposes of advertising or fraud. While risks exist, it is possible to find a happy medium in which one can live online responsibly and

US senator Richard Blumenthal has repeatedly introduced legislation to regulate digital privacy alongside other members of Congress.

safely but still maintain some control over what information is shared and how it is used.

If information is stored insecurely, this collected data can become susceptible to a data breach, or unauthorized access to view or copy the information. With so many users online and such a large volume of data being recorded on each user, data breaches have become common. Although a data breach can be a signal to update passwords and be on the alert for suspicious activity, not all users understand the severity of having their personal information stolen. What's more, companies may try to cover up or trivialize such an event. In 2014, hackers stole account information, including user names, passwords, and personal information, for more than five hundred million Yahoo! users. The breach was not revealed to users or the public for two years.

MYTHS AND FACTS

MYTH: I can edit or delete my Facebook and Twitter posts if I later change my mind about what I wrote. No one will know the difference because it exists only in that one place.

FACT: In some cases, posts can be edited or even deleted, but doing so will have no impact on anyone who has already read it. In some cases, changes to a post that has already been shared will impact only the original copy. For instance, a deleted tweet will still exist as any retweets it received. Furthermore, the social media site, third-party web archives, and search engines can record this content and make it publicly searchable the moment the post is made. Anything posted to the internet really can stick around forever.

MYTH: I can remain anonymous when using apps and websites that don't require an account.

FACT: These apps may not ask for a name, password, or credit card info, but they can still retain a device's internet protocol (IP) address and its general location. Websites often store hidden tracking cookies that can be used to report how often you visit and at what times. All of this info can be used to build a profile that is used when showing ads or displaying content, or it can even be passed along to other services.

(continued on the next page)

(continued from the previous page)

MYTH: I don't need to worry about my privacy online because I have nothing to hide.

FACT: Cyberbullies enjoy harassing others online, regardless of who they are. Identity thieves value your personal info, including name and age. You don't necessarily need to have a credit card or bank account to become a target. Additionally, with unlimited tracking of your activities, a classmate, teacher, or parent could look over music or a movie you have streamed and become offended—entirely unintentionally. In order to think freely, your online activities require just as much privacy as your offline activities.

CHAPTER THREE

A MODERN APPROACH TO PRIVACY PROTECTION

Protecting one's digital privacy doesn't have to be a distraction, but it does require awareness and diligence. Knowing how to safely and securely navigate websites and apps can create a more fulfilling experience. These techniques can also better prepare you for changes in technology as digital privacy awareness grows and different threats transform.

THE KEY TO PASSWORDS

Website administrators are well aware of the fact that the first line of protection for any information system is the password. More and more websites now require a decent level of complexity in the password when creating an account. However, it is difficult—if not impossible—to be sure the password is saved securely and encrypted to keep it inaccessible. But there is a way for users to protect themselves. Use a unique password for each site that requires an account. This way, if a password for one site does become compromised, then passwords for other sites won't automatically be compromised as well. Similarly, using the same email address or user name for many accounts makes it easy for someone to hack into multiple services, so these also shouldn't be constant from one site to the next. But one measure to protect an account that may rely on using the same information is taking advantage of two-factor authentication. Also called 2FA or TFA, it establishes an additional and perhaps variable piece of identifying information that the user must supply in order to sign in.

A number of password-manager software solutions are available to handle and vary passwords. Not only

Multifactor authentication is a free source of security that users can implement on their own if a website has a mechanism for activating it.

do these store your passwords so that you don't need to remember or even type them all, they also generate new passwords. Generated passwords can meet different levels of complexity, such as password length and the ratio between letters, numbers, and special characters. Password managers can report on the level of security provided by each password and help identify cases of password reuse. To keep this data safe, password managers encrypt all of the entered information and lock it behind a single master password or biometric lock, such as a fingerprint scan using a mobile phone.

An alternative to creating a unique password for each new account you create is to connect a social account, such as Facebook, and sign in using that account. If you trust a social network more than a new site, this is a good option. Connecting a social account provides the benefit of needing to remember only the single password. Using a single sign on (SSO) solution maintains security by never revealing the actual password to the sites and apps being accessed. Additionally, there is often a method to control the authorizations allowed through the account, providing the opportunity to revoke access.

PRIVACY AT HOME

For many, online access occurs most at home. Additionally, home is where many people feel the safest. Digital privacy begins at home as well, with responsible browser usage and safe online access. Using your own computer at home allows you a great range of options in configuring the settings.

A good first step is to ensure the computer has reliable antivirus software that is installed, running, and up-to-date before going online. Newer operating systems often include antivirus software, though many alternatives can be found for free, including Avast, AVG, and Bitdefender. Once installed, antivirus software will monitor the computer and online activity to watch for spyware and malware, as well as potentially harmful websites and phishing attempts. The software regularly checks for updates, but it is a best practice to check for and install an update manually at least once a month, if one is available.

When using a web browser, it can be beneficial to install a few plug-ins for enhanced privacy and safety. An ad blocker prevents advertising from being shown within websites and can also reduce the amount of personal information and activity reported to these ad services. To ensure all data is communicated securely, at least when possible, use a plug-in like HTTPS Everywhere to use an encrypted connection by default when it can. It warns the user when it can't so the risk is apparent.

Though today's browsers often include a privacy or anonymous mode, it can be limited. A more robust alternative is to use a tracking blocker such as Disconnect or Ghostery. These work by limiting what cookie data is created and stored on your computer by the browser and what data can be tracked through the browser. As with ad blockers, limiting traffic associated with tracking also reduces the network usage and can speed up your online experience.

AdBlock is an extension that prevents all ads from appearing. Apps like this can prevent malicious code from running, and they can prevent invasive or offensive imagery from appearing on a webpage.

PRIVACY AT SCHOOL

When using a public computer at school or a library, you likely will not be able to verify that antivirus software is installed or that it has safely removed any dangers. Similarly, you may not be able to install any software, including browser plug-ins. For these situations, common sense can be the best defense. It doesn't hurt to ask the information technology (IT) department about how vigorous computer security is. Whatever the answer, if you have reason to suspect that the computer may not be safe to use, don't use it. If you have access to another device that you have more control over, such as a smartphone, using that may be a safer alternative (if its use is permitted).

Most threats try not to make their presence known, and spyware or keylogging software could be recording and reporting everything you do—including entering passwords—without you realizing it. A good course of action is to limit your activity on the public computer to what is anonymous. Search the library catalog, view class notes, and complete assigned materials. Avoid entering any personal information, including your phone number, address, and passwords. There is probably already a usage policy in place that gives guidelines for what is permitted when at the computer, which will help maintain a distraction-free environment and protect your privacy.

PRIVACY ON THE GO (MOBILE DEVICES)

Your phone is a personal device, so to avoid inputting personal information into it would be counter to its purpose. But portable devices can be lost or invaded easily if one is not cautious. As with any secure account, protect your phone with a strong password. Don't use obvious sequences like your date of birth or name. Activating fingerprint reading as a means of protection is another great option for enhancing your phone's security. The device should be set to auto-lock after

This phone is displaying its lock screen. Security options for a device like this range from passwords and PINs to biometrics and remote erasing, and they all protect content stored on the device.

one or two minutes of being inactive so that attempting to unlock it will initiate the need to enter the password. And be sure to share only fairly impersonal notifications and information on the lock screen. Consider it as public knowledge—the content there could be seen by anybody. These quick steps will help prevent unwanted access and can keep your information private if the phone becomes lost or stolen.

App usage is the other big-ticket item when it comes to managing privacy on your mobile phone. Before installing an unfamiliar app is the best time to evaluate

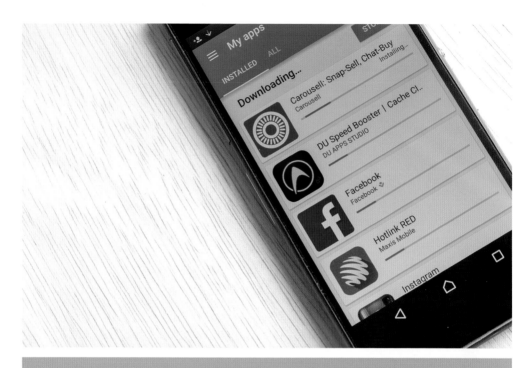

Some apps update themselves without seeking permission each time. Updates drain data, but they also implement recent security changes and fixes.

whether or not it can do any damage. Check its release date, reviews, developer, and permissions. Apps that have just recently been released do not have the benefit of the test of time. Similarly, an old app without any reviews points to an app no one is willing to use. Finally, some apps are created to look like, or spoof, a respected app in order to gain trust and installs. Verifying the developer should allow you to be sure the app is what you are expecting—some reviews reveal fakes, too. Some devices, notably Android phones, will provide a preview of what permissions the app requests upon install. This preview is an indicator of what type of

SOCIAL SHARING PRIVACY CHECKLIST

Own your privacy settings. Before sharing, review your settings so that posts are viewable only by friends, rather than being entirely public.

Maintain your friendships. Your friend list should be just that: a list of friends. Users you don't know or don't feel comfortable sharing with don't belong there.

Think before you share. Once your post is made, it is likely it can never truly be removed or undone. Be certain that what you're saying can't get you into trouble.

Choose your tags wisely. Tagging posts can be a fun way to include others and note your location. Doing so can also unintentionally make your post visible to a wider audience.

Check in often. Social networks and the technology they are built on change rapidly. Watch for privacy policy and feature updates, and don't hesitate to ask an adult for help understanding what these changes might mean for you.

information the app will be able to access. If you are in doubt, it is best to assume that the app is not safe.

During use, it's a good idea to regularly check the device settings and be aware of what apps are doing in the background when they're not actively being used. Anything suspicious is a candidate for immediate uninstall. When it is time to upgrade to a new device, be sure to follow your manufacturer's instructions for removing all personal data from the phone before you part with it.

STAYING PRIVATE WHILE GOING SOCIAL

When interacting socially on a website or app, the element of real-time communication can complicate privacy management. In this arena, all of the guidelines noted above apply, but now with a very real audience. First and foremost, don't say or post anything you may later regret. When sharing online, you should know your audience, but also consider that this audience may have users you don't know personally. Don't overshare. You may accidentally insult someone, or someone may take your post out of context and share it with an even broader audience. Even when communicating privately, a personal photo or phone number could become public through any number of ways outside of your control.

The competitive environment of online gaming can bring playful taunts to the level of personal insult and shouting matches. Developers usually integrate a means to block belligerent players or report them if you feel harassed. At the other end of the spectrum, others with whom you often play may become good friends. Still, keeping these friendships within the game world is the safest course of action. Never share personal information with people you don't know in the offline world.

TEN GREAT QUESTIONS TO ASK A CYBERSECURITY SPECIALIST

1. My friends want me to download a new social networking app. How do I know if it's safe?
2. Is it safer to connect to Facebook or another social networking site using a browser or an app?
3. How do my risks change when using a public computer at the school library?
4. Is it safer to connect to the internet on a phone over a cellular or Wi-Fi connection?
5. What form of two-factor authentication is best to use?
6. Are public Wi-Fi networks safe to use?
7. Is password-generation and management software safe to use?
8. How often should I change my passwords?
9. Is it safe to allow my web browser to save account and address information?
10. How can I be sure my information is kept private after it leaves my device?

CHAPTER FOUR

RECOVERING FROM PRIVACY CRIMES

P ersonal privacy is highly valued, but it is often overlooked until it has been invaded. Having to deal with credit card charges in your name that you didn't make, personal photos or comments shared with the world, or someone impersonating you online and defaming you can have a long-term impact. It is important to treat such acts for what they are: a crime. Becoming the victim of a digital privacy crime can leave someone feeling broken and powerless, but there are steps that can be taken to ensure safety and recovery.

The legal system is continuing to update and better address digital crimes of all types to best help victims recover and continue living a normal life. A special focus has been applied to aiding victims under age eighteen. In fact, at the start of 2015, the state of California enacted its Online Eraser law, which gives minors the right to remove content they have posted to any online service using their account. It is inevitable that we will see more of this type of legislation and expanded digital privacy rights.

DON'T GO IT ALONE

After becoming the victim of a digital privacy crime, the first step is to seek help. Immediately reach out to a parent or another adult worthy of trust. Despite the situation, it's vital to stay calm, and having someone to help and provide emotional and practical support will enable that. It is important to have someone who is approachable and who is in a position to help directly. Additionally, depending on the situation, a parent who is also a victim of the crime may need to freeze bank accounts or contact the credit bureaus to report the crime.

When facing an invasion of privacy, a vital first step is to discuss what happened with a trusted adult who can help support you emotionally and practically.

Next, reach out to the police. It is common to want to play off the attack as bad luck or a one-time problem, but the police are there specifically to respond to crimes. Having them deal with the crime means less worry and work trying to fix it for the victim. Police have access to resources for addressing the crime and avoiding further incidents. Working with the police early will allow the victim to identify the best steps to stop the crime and begin recovery, and it may even help other victims.

CYBERBULLYING AND ABUSE

Cyberabuse can take many forms. It can be a bully looking to get an irritated response out of you; someone picking on you because of race, gender, or sexual orientation; or someone obsessed to the point of stalking you. However it manifests, it is an invasion of privacy that can be difficult to stop.

Safety should be the primary goal of any action that attempts to deal with cyberabuse. If a user feels physically threatened or thinks that there may be a potential for physical threat, the user should not respond or retaliate. In many cases, a response may lead to further harassment—but this is not the same as causing the harassment. If a threat seems imminent, get out of there: find a safe place to be with a parent or trusted adult. Users may be able to block and ban abusers on social networks to prevent the person from contacting them. Some services, including Twitter, include a separate option for muting a user. Muting hides communications and posts without sharing the status of being muted with the muted individual. And informing a site administrator of the abuse can get the administrator to help end it.

It is a good idea to document the abuse by saving chat logs, emails, and messages. Records will aid in any investigation or legal proceedings that may occur, or it may just show a site administrator that the problem is real. If a Save option is not immediately available, saving a screenshot can work just as well. Be sure to record the date of each incident if it's not included with the log. Even if you don't think you will seek legal recourse, having the harassment logged can be helpful if it ever escalates or returns in the future.

ACCOUNT HIJACKING AND IMPERSONATION

Attempting to log in to a social network only to find that someone has changed the password can cause frustration, anger, and annoyance. It can also expand to identity theft and harassment. To help contain the problem, secure any other accounts by changing the passwords and security questions. Be sure to reach out to the service's support organization to have the account frozen and the password reset. If there are any bank or purchase accounts linked to the hijacked account, continue to monitor for unexpected activity.

Similarly, users may encounter someone impersonating them online. Rather than accessing an account directly, an imposter may steal and repost a user's photos and content and attempt to fool others into thinking that he

Actor Derek Luke is one of many celebrities to be impersonated online. In his case, the fake Instagram account for him gained thousands of followers by sharing fake life events.

or she is the user. Regardless of how mild the imperson-ator's actions are—simply reposting a user's materials and trying to realistically emulate that person's personality— the impersonator is probably breaking site regulations and should have his or her account shut down.

In both cases, users should save screenshots and logs to document any posts or updates made by the attacker. These will be necessary when contacting support and may be useful to the police or legal agencies. Users should also warn friends who may be impacted by the attacker so that they don't engage in communication or share information.

IDENTITY THEFT

Identity theft can have long-term effects that impact someone's credit report and criminal record. It can make it difficult to create a bank account or apply for a loan, apply for college, and obtain a job—even years after the incident. If not halted, the attacker can and will continue to damage the target's reputation. If you become the victim of identity theft, you should immediately contact the police and work with your parents to reach out to any impacted accounts. This may include your bank, the Social Security Administration, your state's Department of Motor Vehicles, and your cell phone carrier.

The police and other agencies will provide additional steps for reporting the identity theft, which vary depend-ing on the specifics of the crime. You will need to provide copies of fraudulent activity and purchases so you should continue to log any suspicious activity you find. If the attacker created accounts and made purchases under your name, it may spark calls from debt collection agencies. If it comes to this, record these calls and reach out to the credit reporting agencies. You may need to reach out to the Federal Trade Commission (FTC) to report the erroneous debt reports if your credit report is not corrected.

STOLEN DEVICES AND DATA LEAKS

You should report a stolen or lost mobile device to the police. Alert your mobile carrier next so that it can

WHEN BIG DATA GOES BIGGER

As users do more and more online, the amount of user data being gathered and stored online increases. These depositories—which contain a wealth of personal information ranging from names, addresses, and emails to credit card and Social Security numbers—are a frequent target for hackers. The stolen data is often sold on the black market, which by some estimates has become more lucrative than the illegal drug trade.

In late 2015, VTech, a maker of digital toys and software for children, had its user data server hacked. Hackers were able to steal personal information on more than five million users, including the names, gender, and birth dates of children. This data, along with the billing and personal info of the children's parents, could be used to attach a physical address to each child. This marked the first major data breach to directly impact children.

freeze the device and correct any expenses. The carrier may be able to track the phone using the Global Positioning System (GPS), which can aid in the police investigation. If you have the ability to remotely erase the device, you should consider this as an option as well.

When personal data is stolen as a result of a data breach, there may not be an alert or any suspicious activity for some time, possibly never. If you suspect any of your account information was associated with a mass data breach, first update all potentially impacted passwords and then watch for suspicious activity. If credit card information

Fast action is important when dealing with identity theft or financial fraud. It's best to contact any banking institutions directly by phone.

may have been included with the compromised account information, contact the credit lenders to request a new card. Usually, the company that was attacked provides a method of contact for potential victims to find out more about what steps they should follow and what information was stolen.

CHAPTER FIVE

TAKING ACTION

After becoming the victim of a cyberattack, confronting the problem is only the first step in moving on. The psychological damage of such a breach can lead to mistrust, anxiety and depression, and even suicide. Rebuilding one's life and trust is a challenge, but some techniques exist that can help manage the burden of recovering safely to lead a healthy lifestyle and online presence.

EMOTIONAL RECOVERY

Becoming the victim of a crime is an emotional event, and it's normal to have strong emotions stemming from it like anger, frustration, and embarrassment. Everyone's experience is different, and everyone's recovery will be equally different. It's important to move at your own speed and to know that, with time, things will be better. This is another area where having a companion can make a big difference. A source of support that is reliable eases the burden and helps avoid or alleviate the

Becoming a victim is a serious ordeal, with the emotional and physical impact often lasting much longer than the initial digital impact.

sense of being singled out by the attack. One option for support that can create positivity is to join local advocacy groups, which exist to help those in recovery and to identify connections to additional resources.

If you are recovering from a crime against your digital privacy, it's important to remember you are a victim and that this was a crime. It's not your fault, and you are not to blame. It's natural to feel mistrust and embarrassment, but these feelings do go away. Remember that you are important and there are people who do truly care about you, so be sure to reach out to them.

PHYSICAL RECOVERY

Rebuilding oneself as part of recovery can be exhausting, and overcoming the stress involved requires attention to one's physical as well as emotional state. Stress is a very real and often crippling state in which your body attempts to respond to overwhelming circumstances with a fight-or-flight mentality. Stress can cause symptoms such as poor or shallow breathing, difficulty sleeping, headaches, and pressure or pain in your chest. It can reduce the ability to focus and can increase irritability. It's easy to see how the great amount of stress created by a severe invasion of one's privacy can incapacitate someone and create a snowball-like effect that can feel impossible to escape.

At its heart, stress is a physical reaction. Thankfully, this also means that taking care of oneself physically can have a very real and lasting effect to diminish stress. Figure out how to relax. Simply taking time for yourself and focusing on relaxing and breathing can help reduce stress. If you find yourself showing symptoms of stress, or someone close to you shows concern, first try to breathe deeply and steadily. This process can help signal to your brain that things are okay, which allows the rest of your body to follow suit.

Another great choice to reduce stress is exercise. Playing sports with friends, taking a walk, or working out can help combat the effects of stress. You may also find that adjusting your diet to include fruits and vegetables, complemented by protein-rich foods, can have a big impact.

Doing yoga and going to relaxing places are great ways to deal with stress. It's the beginning of enabling oneself to move beyond a traumatic experience.

Other recommended foods include yogurt, oatmeal, milk, and even dark chocolate. If you have a strong craving for something a little less healthy, it can be good to give in to that craving, as long as you do so in moderation.

During the recovery process, don't try to make any big changes overnight. Reducing stress is something that needs to be done over time.

BECOME AN ADVOCATE

One of the best ways to maintain your own privacy in the digital age is to encourage those around you to do

TAKING ADVANTAGE OF PRIVACY CONCERNS

As online users become more aware of their digital privacy, some people look to twist these concerns into hysteria and confusion. Since 2009, a privacy hoax has occasionally appeared on the popular social network Facebook claiming that its privacy policies have changed. Specifically, the scam reports that Facebook will now own all messages and media shared through the site. It asks that users include a legal clause somewhere within their posts to allow them to retain ownership of them.

While this message is entirely false, it has repeatedly caused confusion and mistrust within Facebook's network. The message has earned enough attention that it has been shared and obtained viral status multiple times. Though it may not have done any real harm, it hasn't done much to help educate users on the very real privacy concerns they should be focusing on.

the same. Being an advocate doesn't have to mean attending rallies and writing letters to Congress—even just small reminders to friends and family about how they can improve their digital privacy can stimulate big changes. If you see a friend share something that looks suspect or observe behavior that might indicate cyberabuse, say something to that friend discreetly. Encourage others to care about their privacy and to understand the risks that are present. Explain and demonstrate how to properly and safely choose and use social media and mobile apps. In many cases, simply understanding how a digital footprint is created and how the decisions one makes can impact it, can steer behavior toward adopting a healthier approach to computer and mobile phone usage.

Similarly, remain vigilant for changes to privacy policies and the laws behind them. Understand that this technology continues to grow and that the ways we maintain our privacy will evolve with it. As an advocate, you accept the responsibility to set a positive example for others in how you choose to use your phone, what information you choose to share online, and how effectively you create and manage your digital footprint.

If you are a victim and are comfortable sharing your experience, you may consider discussing with friends or classmates the challenges you faced in overcoming the cybercrime. If you are not comfortable talking openly, you may find the private setting of a support group, where other victims can find strength in your words, to be a positive venue for sharing. Another option is to maintain a journal to record your progress and struggles privately. This journal can be used as a reminder of that progress or even as a reference should you want to speak publicly at a later time.

MOVING FORWARD

Digital privacy continues to be in the spotlight, with recent evidence including the iPhone encryption debate held between the Federal Bureau of

Investigation (FBI) and Apple and security concerns over Hillary Clinton's private email server. It's only natural that we will see new and improved legislation to handle these new risks.

One such attempt at enacting legislation is the Intimate Privacy Protection Act, a bill that was proposed in Congress in 2016. The act aims to make it a crime to distribute sexually explicit materials of a visual nature (photos, videos, or other media) that were intended to be private. Under the new law, anyone found sharing the images without permission would be guilty of a crime.

But such attempts to fix the wrongs of invaded privacy will be effective only with the vigilant observance of all users. The best protection an internet user can put to use will be knowing how to deal with the situations that are likely to appear.

analytics Data collection and analysis used to identify patterns, typically used to record anonymous information on website and app users.

anonymous Remaining unknown and sharing no personally identifying information.

antivirus Describing software used to protect users from and remove harmful computer programs.

cookie A small amount of information stored within a web browser by a visited server, often to track user activity or statistics.

data breach Unauthorized access to sensitive/private information, often resulting in the theft of information.

data collection The gathering of information, such as user demographics and personal traits, with the intent to measure it.

digital privacy The boundaries that define what a person can represent, access, or hide about himself or herself or others while online.

encryption The conversion of data into a format that is intentionally unreadable by anyone other than the intended audience.

information technology (IT) A division of an organization that works to ensure the availability and security of digital resources.

keylogging Recording input by a computer user to a malicious piece of software, typically without the user's knowledge.

malware Software created with the intent to do damage to the computers it is run on.

password A string of characters meant to be kept secret, used to access protected information and systems.

phishing Mimicking a legitimate organization to trick users into providing sensitive information.

privacy The limited right to not be intruded upon in one's personal or professional life.

server A computer that allows access to content or services to other computers over a network.

single sign on (SSO) A method of logging in to multiple services by signing in to one account.

spoof Imitating another piece of software or service with the intent to trick the end user.

spyware Software that gathers data and information from a computer without the user's knowledge.

two-factor authentication (2FA or TFA) An added layer of security attached to an account log-in that relies on an outside form of identification, such as a text message.

Wi-Fi A network access created for wireless devices, such as smartphones and computers.

Canadian Anti-Fraud Centre
PO Box 686
North Bay, ON P1B 8J8
Canada
(888) 495-8501
Website: http://www.antifraudcentre.ca
This organization handles fraud and information related
    to fraud within Canada. It provides education and
    information to prevent fraud, as well as providing
    support to law enforcement agencies.

Consumer Measures Committee
c/o Office of Consumer Affairs
Industry Canada
235 Queen Street, 6th Floor W.
Ottawa, ON K1A 0H5
Canada
(613) 943-2502
Website: http://cmcweb.ca/eic/site/cmc-cmc.nsf/eng
    /home
The Consumer Measures Committee works with provin-
    cial governments to improve the consumer market-
    place by updating regulations and raising aware-
    ness of fraud-related risk.

Electronic Frontier Foundation
815 Eddy Street
San Francisco, CA 94109
(415) 436-9333

Website: https://www.eff.org

This foundation advocates for civil liberties in the modern digital world. The group works with specialists and experts to fight for free speech online and to defend the privacy of the digital community.

Electronic Privacy Information Center (EPIC)

1718 Connecticut Avenue NW, Suite 200
Washington, DC 20009
(202) 483-1140
Website: https://epic.org

This research center provides public education and regularly speaks before Congress and courts on matters impacting digital privacy and civil liberties.

Federal Trade Commission (FTC)

600 Pennsylvania Avenue NW
Washington, DC 20580
(202) 326-2222
Website: https://www.ftc.gov

The FTC addresses business practices that are unfair to consumers, including deceptive or anticompetitive activities, and it works to protect consumers' digital privacy rights.

Internet Society

1775 Wiehle Avenue, Suite 201
Reston, VA 20190-5108
(703) 439-2120
Website: https://www.internetsociety.org

This society is a recognized leader in internet policy and standards.

WEBSITES

Because of the changing nature of internet links, Rosen Publishing has developed an online list of websites related to the subject of this book. This site is updated regularly. Please use this link to access this list:

http://www.rosenlinks.com/NTKL/privacy

Currie, Stephen. *Online Privacy*. San Diego, CA: Refer-
  encePoint Press, 2011.
Fromm, Megan. *Privacy and Digital Security*. New York,
  NY: Rosen Publishing Group, 2015.
Giles, Lamar. *Endangered*. New York, NY: Harp-
  erTeen, 2015.
Grayson, Robert. *Managing Your Digital Footprint*. New
  York, NY: Rosen Publishing Group, 2011.
Jacobs, Thomas. *What Are My Rights?* Minneapolis,
  MN: Free Spirit Publishing, 2011.
Mayrock, Aija. *The Survival Guide to Bullying: Written
  by a Teen*. New York, NY: Scholastic, 2015.
Merino, Noel. *Teen Rights and Freedoms: Privacy*. San
  Diego, CA: Greenhaven Press, 2012.
Meyer, Terry Teague. *Careers in Computer Forensics*.
  New York, NY: Rosen Publishing Group, 2014.
Stead, Rebecca. *Goodbye Stranger*. New York, NY:
  Wendy Lamb Books, 2015.
Suen, Anastasia. *Online Privacy and the Law*. New
  York, NY: Rosen Publishing Group, 2012.
Wilkinson, Colin. *Gaming: Playing Safe and Playing
  Smart*. New York, NY: Rosen Publishing Group, 2011.

Anderson, Monica. "6 Facts About Americans and Their Smartphones." Pew Research Center. Retrieved October 16, 2016. http://www.pewresearch.org/fact-tank/2015/04/01/6-facts-about-americans-and-their-smartphones.

Bronskill, Jim, and David McKie. *Your Right to Privacy: Minimize Your Digital Footprint.* Bellingham, WA: Self-Counsel Press, 2016.

Cullen, Terri. *The Wall Journal. Complete Identity Theft Guidebook.* New York, NY: Three Rivers Press, 2007.

Internet Live Stats. "Internet Users." Retrieved October 16, 2016. http://www.internetlivestats.com/internet-users.

Kelley, Michael B. "NSA: Snowden Stole 1.7 MILLION Classified Documents and Still Has Access to Most of Them." Business Insider. Retrieved October 16, 2016. http://www.businessinsider.com/how-many-docs-did-snowden-take-2013-12.

Kroft, Steve. "The Data Brokers: Selling Your Personal Information." CBS News. Retrieved October 10, 2016. http://www.cbsnews.com/news/the-data-brokers-selling-your-personal-information/.

Leiner, Barry M. "Brief History of the Internet." Internet Society. Retrieved October 11, 2016. http://www.internetsociety.org/internet/what-internet/history-internet/brief-history-internet.

Mendelsohn, Tom. "Yahoo Investigating Claimed Breach and Data Dump of 200 Million Users." Ars Technica. Retrieved October 16, 2016. http://

arstechnica.com/security/2016/08/yahoo-email-data
-breach-dump.

Moore, Alexis, and Laurie J. Edwards. *Cyber Self-Defense: Expert Advice to Avoid Online Predators, Identity Theft, and Cyberbullying.* Guilford, CT: Lyons Press, 2014.

Morris, Jason, and Ed Lavandera. "Why Big Companies Buy, Sell Your Data." CNN. Retrieved October 10, 2016. http://www.cnn.com/2012/08/23/tech/web/big-data-acxiom.

Nisen, Max. "These Charts Show What We're Not Doing Because We're Online All the Time." Business Insider. Retrieved October 16, 2016. http://www.businessinsider.com/how-much-time-people-spend-online-2013-10.

Payton, Theresa M., and Theodore Claypoole. *Privacy in the Age of Big Data: Recognizing Threats, Defending Your Rights, and Protecting Your Family.* Lanham, MD: Rowman & Littlefield, 2014.

Pew Research Center. "Americans Going Online … Explosive Growth, Uncertain Destinations." Retrieved October 11, 2016. http://www.people-press.org/1995/10/16/americans-going-online-explosive-growth-uncertain-destinations.

Scheer, Robert. *They Know Everything About You: How Data-Collecting Corporations and Snooping Government Agencies Are Destroying Democracy.* New York, NY: Nation Books, 2015.

Schneier, Bruce. *Schneier on Security.* Indianapolis, IN: Wiley Publishing, 2008.

Steyer, James P. *Talking Back to Facebook.* New York, NY: Scribner, 2012.

Victor, Daniel. "Security Breach at Toy Maker VTech Includes Data on Children." New York Times. Retrieved October 11, 2016. http://www.nytimes .com/2015/12/01/business/security-breach-at-toy-maker-vtech-includes-data-on-children.html.

Weisman, Steve. *Identity Theft Alert: 10 Rules You Must Follow to Protect Yourself from America's #1 Crime.* Upper Saddle River, NJ: FT Press, 2015.

Zakon, Robert H. "Hobbes' Internet Timeline 23." Zakon.org. Retrieved October 11, 2016. http://www.zakon.org/robert/internet/timeline.

ABOUT THE AUTHOR

Colin Wilkinson is a seventeen-year veteran of the video games industry, where he creates a blend of educational and entertainment titles for kids. He has contributed to numerous games involving online components designed to add safe and private experiences for children. Wilkinson has also worked developing user-centric social websites and services for the cloud. He lives on a small dairy farm with his wife and two children.

PHOTO CREDITS

Cover Yuri Arcurs/DigitalVision/Getty Images; p. 5 dennizn/Shutterstock.com; pp. 7, 16, 27, 38, 46 Maksim Kabakou/Shutterstock.com; p. 9 James Leynse/Corbis Historical/Getty Images; p. 11 Rob Crandall/Shutterstock.com; p. 13 Frederick M. Brown/Getty Images; p. 15 Hero Images/Getty Images; p. 17 Justin Sullivan/Getty Images; p. 19 Lester Lefkowitz/The Image Bank/Getty Images; p. 22 Thailand Photos for Sale/Shutterstock.com; p. 23 Chip Somodevilla/Getty Images; p. 28 Bill Hinton/Moment Mobile/Getty Images; p. 31 Monika Skolimowska/picture-alliance/dpa/AP Images; p. 33 Wachiwit/Shutterstock.com; p. 34 N. Azlin Sha/Shutterstock.com; p. 39 Maskot/Getty Images; p. 42 Michael Tran/FilmMagic/Getty Images; p. 45 Tooga/Stone/Getty Images; p. 47 Justin Paget/Corbis/Getty Images; p. 49 Rock Gomez/Corbis/Getty Images; back cover photo by marianna armata/Moment/Getty Images.

Design: Michael Moy; Layout Design: Tahara Anderson
Editor: Bernadette Davis; Photo Research: Nicole Baker